Motivating From Within

"Possessing Inner Wisdom To Change"

Lavette Willis-Crittenton

Motivating From Within Copyright © April 2016 by
Lavette Willis-Crittenton

Published in the United States of America by
Gospel 4 U Publishing

All rights reserved. No part of this book may be reproduced or transmitted in anyway by means, electronic, mechanical, Photocopy, recording or otherwise, without prior permission of the author except as provided by USA copyright law.

Scriptures are taken from the King James Version unless otherwise marked.

ISBN - 9780692648476

Library of Congress Control Number: 2016934292

Printed in United States of America
April 2016

Content

DEDICATION
FOREWORD
ACKNOWLEDGEMENT
INTRODUCTION

1. The Mirror Image 17
2. The Mask 31
3. Depression 43
4. Acceptance 57
5. Forgiveness 69
6. Change 77
7. Loving Yourself 91
8. Trusting Yourself 105
9. Trusting Others 121
10. Free 137

LAVETTE WILLIS-CRITTENTON

Dedication

I would like to dedicate *Motivating From Within* to a few very special people who have been my greatest inspirations in life. First, to my beautiful daughters Ashley Bryant and Michelle Willis, who have always been my pride and joy. My most precious gifts from God; you ladies have been my heart and soul - the very air I breathe. I will forever love you to the moon and back again; being your mother has been my highest accomplishment in life. My every dream was to make you ladies proud to have me as your mother; you have been my encouragement and my will to be the best example of what a woman should be. I love you both with all my heart; there would be no me, without the two of you. Love you forever, your MOMMIE.

To my Great Grandmother; may God bless her exquisite soul, Mary Lee Liggins. The woman who believed in me when I didn't believe in myself; you saw the potential and planted the seeds which gave me the desire to search for wisdom. Your strength and determination to succeed was the best gift you instilled in me and I was blessed to have a woman so unselfish, love me endlessly. For your love, knowledge and support I thank you. I will forever hold you in my heart - I love you Grandma May, "This one's for you"

Love Always Pooh

Foreword

I am free, praise the Lord! I'm free, and no longer bound. No more chains are holding me. This easy-to-read, powerful, full-of-hope, destiny-seeking, and victory-filled book is a must read. As you flip through the pages of this book, a window is opened up so that all past hurt and pain can be thrown out. While at the same time, fresh air is blown in for your new start.

This is a book about truth. It acknowledges that God has to be part of the process, and forgiveness must be a key component. Lavette totally opens up, leaving herself vulnerable yet free, in an attempt to free others whose past has set out to doom their future. Life sometimes leads us through a dark tunnel but there are promises—light is soon to come if we just endure. Lavette will challenge you to face the skeletons that lay dormant in your closet, screaming to get out and be free. It is a process of identifying, conquering, and defeating.

This is a book for all ages. It addresses life, challenges, and circumstances but ultimately shows victory. It evokes many different emotions. As you read it to the end, you will be able to face childhood abuse, teen pregnancy, drug addiction, abandonment, and more by motivating yourself from within.

Mirror, mirror on the wall who's the fierce of them all? By the end of this book the answer will be: YOU.

Rev. Charlene N. Outterbridge

Youth Pastor

Church of the Living God, SM-Kensington

Acknowledgement

I would like to first give all thanks and glory to God: Thank you, for providing me with the strength and wisdom to see this process through.

LAVETTE WILLIS-CRITTENTON

Introduction

Motivating From Within was inspired by my life experiences. I am not a Doctor or some kind of Professor coming to you with book knowledge and a host of credentials. Although I received my Bachelor's Degree in Business Administration and am currently pursuing a Master's Degree in Informatics; that is not the journey I wish to share. My experience comes from 'life' and by living on life's terms. My personal journey dates back to when I was a young girl; hurt, abandoned, living within the foster care system and running from man to man in search of love and happiness. *Motivating From Within* shares my story of how I began to connect with self-happiness and inner peace. This book summarizes the road I have traveled - along with the tears I have shed, while climbing out of the hole of darkness to see the light of joy. *Motivating From Within* outlines basic steps that most parents and teachers fail to provide our youth in understanding how to proclaim self-satisfaction. *Motivating From Within* may assist individuals of all ages who find themselves repeating the same chapters in life, receiving the same outcome.

This self-help book will inspire individuals to make changes in their lives by identifying underlying issues that we as humans choose to deny. *Motivating From Within* may assist individuals who desire to evaluate the areas in their lives where self-identity has gotten lost within the tangled web of life. This book provides steps I have used personally throughout my life. These steps help me stay true to myself, so that I can make necessary changes in order to continue successfully in the daily battles encountered. *Motivating From Within* provides the ingredients for my inner peace; which leads to self-happiness, growth, satisfaction and success.

I became inspired to write this book by sharing my story with various individuals I met throughout my journey. I realized that people understand the battles and can relate to the message I delivered. So that lead me to believe sharing the secrets of how I fight my battles could help someone who feels alone, or feels clueless as to where and how to find self-satisfaction. I always thought my first book was supposed to be about my life story because I had so many things to share. In the process of writing my story, I stumbled across a roadblock and the word 'stop' appeared in my mind. I prayed repeatedly for God to allow these words to come, but I received nothing. However, one particular night I prayed for God to show me what message He needed me to share and that next morning, I woke up at 6:17am on April 21, 2010; grabbed my notebook and was able to write the outline for this book, *Motivating From Within*. The words began to flow as if someone turned on a faucet of knowledge.

This book is written from my heart and shares the little, detailed ways I began to reclaim my happiness and learned how to motivate myself towards greatness.

Motivating From Within is my story and is what helped me during my journey. Although I know you will find some of these tools useful – remember, there are no scientific experiments performed or 'get rich quick' schemes; only tools I have found useful along my journey to happiness. *Motivating From Within* may provide you with tools to assist you with making positive changes in your life and may also teach individuals how to remain true-to-self for success. Throughout my life, things always seemed to come at me very hard and I never understood why. To this day, I still cannot answer that question; so I stopped trying to make life easier for myself and learned how to motivate myself to deal with tough issues. In life, we learn that we cannot change everything - but we can always change ourselves. In order to maintain successful relationships we change; it's called growth.

While some individuals struggle with this part of life and exhibit what's known as an 'identity crisis' - for me, I felt lost and out of place. If you understand any of my dilemmas, then *Motivating From Within* is the book for you. Today, I live my life happy and satisfied with the decisions I have made and this enables me to possess the self-satisfaction I deserve. I am married and a mother of two healthy, wonderful daughters; a stepmother, a daughter, a sister, a niece - as well as an aunt and friend to many. All of these titles are special to me and fill a massive part of my heart.

What happens to the rest of the heart is what many of us leave unfulfilled; that portion which lacks motivation to achieve our dreams. The portion of your heart life has taken away; the part of your life that hides abuse, anger, frustration, fear and defeat - the part which is unknown to the world and not shared. The part keeping us awake at night; it prevents us from learning to love ourselves, which hinders us from loving others and prevents our growth. Worry no more - you have started the journey of healing, because you may find answers within yourself by applying the methods contained within this book. I anticipate this experience will be useful and hope you choose to apply some, or all of these tools towards your life experiences. As you read my story and apply these methods, life will seem much clearer as you discover self-motivation. Now, let your journey begin.

LAVETTE WILLIS-CRITTENTON

CHAPTER I

THE MIRROR IMAGE

When I look in the mirror, do I love who I see; for all I see is an image of me.

When I look in the mirror, do I love who I be; for all that will be is a vision of me.

This vision I see, is just a shield protecting me, from the hurt and pain which lives inside of thee

As I begin to heal, finally

I see,

The mirror image reveals a product of me.

Now I look in the mirror and I truly can see all the light,

Which shines on me; now

That product of me, is who I see, when I look in the mirror at the image of ME

I can imagine the look on your face as you read this passage, but it must be read with an open mind. The mirror image is a metaphor used to express the things that are over-looked in life. Some may think the mirror is for fixing your hair and make-up; which is true, however when viewing *your life* through the mirror, its purpose changes. The mirror then becomes 'eyes to the soul'. When looking in the mirror, one should use that time to really evaluate their inner truth, which is displayed through how we live our life. The mirror is a reflection of what lives in the heart; these are the things that show in the mirror.

The heart will only hold a limited amount of what we might call 'STUFF'. This stuff - may it be happy or sad, whatever the case; when the heart becomes overwhelmed, the 'stuff' reveals itself in our personality, as well as in our facial expressions. In life, the 'stuff' we hold in our hearts builds walls of protection to assistance us. These walls of protection are known as our coping skills. Each individual we meet in life has a significant impact on us, even when we fail to acknowledge it. Think back to your childhood and try to identify with some of those experiences. My past haunts me in a horrible manner and sometimes I even have panic attacks. The past is not a good place for me but I have learned to deal with my pain in order to move forward. When I remember my childhood I have feelings of abandonment and fear, which have lived within my heart for many years.

Remembering my life as a child, I have few memories of a smiling, playful childhood. When my grandfather passed away, it felt as if my family died with him because tragedy seemed to move in as his body went deeper into the ground. A generation was lost due to the drug epidemic that swept the streets; stealing mothers, fathers, aunts and uncles and leaving young children like me to suffer a horrific life of poverty. That was my life; alone with siblings, struggling to eat and attend school the best we could. It resulted in my siblings and I being placed within the foster care system. Can you imagine the resentment, anger, fear and hurt this can bring on a child? Well I can, because this was the life I lived.

This brief description of my life is for you to see the

image of me; the one I used to see. In my life there was pain and for countless years, I was a product of my environment. I became pregnant at the very early age of 12 to be exact and delivered my first daughter Ashley, at thirteen. No, I do not promote teen pregnancy - but it happens and we must learn not to let our life experiences dictate our future. Remember, God doesn't make mistakes. By the age of fourteen, I had my second daughter Michelle and soon became a high-school dropout. At this point in my life, it was time for me to be an adult; I had two children and two brothers, along with a baby father. Life was indeed hard but I was determined to make it work.

With being under aged and having my brothers, I insisted they stay in school to avoid the hassles of Child Services stepping in. This was my life and it forced me to make a way for us to survive. Although my first daughter's father was with me, we fought like cats and dogs. He drank a lot, causing him to be abusive and I later learned he was experimenting with different drugs, which he kept hidden. Nevertheless, we were a family and together we would make a way. He vowed to always remain a true supporter, raising our children by any means necessary and I must say; he kept his word to never leave us.

Today, he is clean and sober - and a much more pleasant person, might I add. For his commitment and dedication, I will forever love him. This was just some of my 'stuff' I believed was the beginning of an endless journey, which for so many years made me feel like a victim of what I thought was my destiny.

LIFE

Life as I see is painful to me

With no future; only a past that won't

stop haunting me.

Tears and pain which I hold inside prevent me from loving the brightest sunshine, only relief I feel comes from the drugs I inhale, feeling blank and without pain, no anger no hate, only feelings of shame. As I look at my daughters a smile crosses my face; they give me something, but I cannot relate. What is this feeling that tickles me inside, that makes me hold my children with joy and pride, slowly it changes the person I am assumed to be, because my children make me want to become a better me.

At this point in my life, the only joy I had was my children. They were my inspiration my pride and my joy. I placed them on a pedestal because they wiped my tears and held me when I needed to be held. My children were my Gods; the reason I opened my eyes in the morning, the reason I did not slit my wrists in the evenings when I wanted nothing more than to give up on life. My daughters (unbeknownst to them) became the motivation I needed to succeed. Now I know it sounds like a heavy burden for two children to bear and if my burdens caused them any hurt or pain, I do apologize - but at that point in my life I had nothing else to save me. Some individuals think their teen pregnancies are punishments, when in many cases they save our lives.

Many times our children are given to us because we have nothing else to hold on to. They provide the strength and will power that's needed to fight existing battles. They provide love when we need it most; they are gifts from our Heavenly Father. I learned from the wisdom of my great grandmother Mary Liggins (MAY GOD REST HER SOUL); she was the smartest woman I ever encountered and told me to never place anyone above our God. My great grandmother reminded me that if I loved my daughters, to never place them above the LORD. My great grandmother said, "If you love them, don't curse them." At that stage in my life I really did not understand her words; I thought the woman was crazy. My great grandmother explained that we serve a jealous God and when we place people and things above Him and don't give him the glory, He will remove the people and things that blind us. Therefore, at that very moment - my thought process began to shift. I realized I had GOD, even though I did not understand how God could allow innocent children to suffer in such a manner which caused us pain.

I really hated life because it was beating the crap out of me and I was only fourteen - what more could I take? My heart was all cried out; I reached a point where tears no longer fell from my eyes, my heart was hard as stone and I could not feel anything because pain made me cold and numb. Many nights I put my kids to bed and would lay in my bed stoned, praying to God to help me learn how to just stop the pain. Then one day I looked in the mirror and asked myself a simple question, "What do you want out of life?" Strangely, I did not have any answers but I knew I wanted my children to have a better life than the one I had; I knew I wanted to be a better mother than mine was. Nevertheless, my question was how? How do I make life better for them when I was taking my children down the exact same path as my mother had taken me? A path of pain, drugs, abuse and destruction - that to this day, still haunts me. I realized I needed to answer that crazy question; "What do I want?"

I started to pray at night for God to open my eyes and help me see a clear path and lead me into happiness, because this was something I did not understand. I laid there wondering, "Can you hear me GOD?

CAN YOU HEAR ME GOD?

Can you hear me GOD, is what I used to say

I'm screaming and crying trying to release my pain,

Can you hear me GOD is what I used to say,

needing answers and directions just to make it through the day. Can you hear me GOD is what I used to say as I watched the sun go down and another day fade away.

Can you hear me GOD is what I used to say, I no longer want to suffer can you lead the way? Can you hear me GOD is what I used to say as He took my hand to show me the way.

Can you hear me GOD is the ONLY thing I know,

THEN He humbled my heart and His mercy began to show

I do not want you to say, "Oh no not another religious book" - that is not what *Motivating From Within* represents; this passage is to help individuals identify a spiritual connection which must be tapped into for self-healing. The inner connection will enable you to begin loving yourself, opposed to searching for the love of others. Our inner feelings are connected to a higher power. I have not and will never force my beliefs on others; you must choose to find the spirit of God on your own. This is what I believe and you must identify with who or what you believe. Only when an individual can identify with their inner spiritual beliefs, will the emotional hurt be revealed.

As we reveal these emotional layers of hurt, pain, trauma, abuse, neglect, sadness and hate - will all the faces of life begin to show? As these faces appear in our mirror image, questions arise and we begin our search for answers. While these questions are being asked, slowly we realize daily that we respond differently according to each situation. In responding to these situations, we learn to wear the face of life most appropriate in accommodating the problem or issue we need to address. In order to begin the therapeutic process needed for healing, we must learn to be true to self. No matter how hard it becomes, be truthful to you.

When you look in the mirror be totally honest and tell yourself the truth; flaws and all, even when it hurts. Stop lying to yourself and begin the process of staying true to you. Only then will you begin to connect with the person you see in the mirror. Ask yourself, what events occurred to make you feel the need to shield and protect yourself from life? Self-identity my friend, is our first step in the healing process - so start by finding that lost person in the mirror. This coping mechanism is a learned behavior and is what I consider 'the mask of life'. Consequently, this mask we wear covers all the 'ugly' we shield from the world; covering our true feelings until we can no longer identify with self.

In summary, my hope for you in chapter one is that you identify with who you are as a person. Many times, people (including myself) began living a life that was a lie. Today, make a promise moving forward to be truthful to only you. When you look in the mirror, tell yourself exactly who you are at this point in life or you will never see a need to change. We get hurt and carry fear which makes us ugly, however; today the wounds can begin to heal by speaking the truth about your true personality.

Reflections for the Soul

After reading chapter 1, the mirror image allows you time to process the information as it relates to your life. Stop and think about the person you represent for the world to see, then allow yourself time to be honest about who you are and identify your areas of truth which need growth. Self-identity is a major component in the growth process; now is the time to use your mirror to view the key elements keeping you in bondage. As you reflect on your image, take notes and challenge yourself to work through self-improvement to rebuild the person within. I have provided a few starter questions to help you begin the healing process of connecting with the mirror image of self-identity.

Reflection Questions

1. Explain how you see yourself as a person - good or bad. Take a moment for self-examination.

2. How do you believe others see you as a person? Evaluate yourself among men and women. What are the different responses you receive?

3. Why do you have this reflection of yourself? Who were the individuals you believe contributed to your personality traits?

4. Do you like the person staring back at you?
5. Do you feel there is a need for change or improvement within?
6. Do you want to make an effort to change?

LAVETTE WILLIS-CRITTENTON

CHAPTER II
THE MASK

You say you know me, how could this be, when I wear a mask that no one can see

You say you love me, how could this be, when I wear a mask that no one can see

You say you need me, in what way I don't know, when I wear a mask so my feelings won't show

You say your love will always be true, how this could be, when I wear a mask that no one can see

You say all these words with lust in your eyes as you fail to wait for my loving prize

You say you want to kiss away all my pain, but I hide

LAVETTE WILLIS-CRITTENTON

behind the mask that shields my shame

You say your love is always so true, but behind the mask, I'm black and blue

You say all these words from the very start, but slowly our love is drifting apart, as I begin to learn the person who lives within me, behind the mask I can slowly see

All the evil and resentment that dwells in me

As I remove the mask I ask myself who, WHO could this be, because removing the mask allows me to see

Behind the mask is only me

Once again, hiding the pain, more to add to the hurt and shame

You say you know me, how could this be, when I wear a mask that no one can see

You say you love me, how could this be, when I wear a mask that no one can see

Removing the mask because I want to be free, removing the mask so now I can see

Behind the mask, hey world

IT'S ME!!!!

I introduce the mask because in life, we adapt to our environment and in the process of adapting to our environment; we change and respond accordingly. Our lifestyle and character are slowly altered and form the person who fits the existing situation. However, because these changes transpire in such small increments - we fail to acknowledge the changes are even occurring. The many faces of the mask we wear become a large part of our personality and what we present to the world. These are the faces we wear to protect us in times of harm and comfort us in times of sorrow. These masks are considered our coping skills. Coping skills tell us to fight or take flight.

I have noticed over the years that most people - including myself, always claim, "That's just me", when in many cases that is not who we are. It is the behavior that fits our situation and who we have learned to become. When I started evaluating my life, I noticed certain behaviors in me changed with the company I kept. To help you understand, I will share examples of things I had to evaluate in order to understand some of my mood-altering circumstances. In the early hours, I needed to be a mother to my children; I would get up and cook, clean up the girls and get them off to school, but I noticed my voice was different. I spoke differently. I listened to my girls, helped them with homework and it felt good. I was patient and loving; I could laugh and enjoy just being a mother.

After my girls went to school however, my role changed into one of the many masks that I wore. This meant that my attitude changed. The streets required me to be someone outside of me. The mask in the streets needed to be tough, rough and ready for anything. While in my street mask, I was a mean hustler out to get mine. In my street state of mind, I would fight, hustle - even rob a man if I needed to and the friends I maintained agreed with this life style? These friends are the individuals who co-signed my behaviors; we understood the code of the streets. My disposition changed and my thought process changed. I smoked weed, cussed like a sailor and had no feelings for the next man.

Nevertheless, in order to support my street life I needed suppliers. So again my mask changed, chasing the hands on the ticking clock. In the evening hours I needed to be sexy, out-going and seductive to find my next victim. The streets are hard, so my walk was different. My conversation was different, like an animal stalking their next prey as I roamed from bar to bar in search of my next man. My evening mask needed to have confidence, listening skills, smarts and wisdom to attract any man who could supply my needs on the streets. I walked with more attitude than ten of the most exotic women; in my mind there was no man walking the face of the earth I could not conquer.

My evening mask was seductive, sensual, conniving and cunning; everyman's dream and nightmare all packaged to perfection. Afterwards, I was left with a mask that wanted nothing more than to have a close-nit family; so I cooked, cleaned and made sure we had Thanksgiving dinner, Christmas dinner and all the closeness a family could share with little knowledge of what a family should be.

While wearing these various masks, my life (in my opinion) was always okay, because in my mind my life was mimicking the Cosby Show. In this version of my life, everything was good; I became the perfect mother with my children's father, my brothers and my girls. We lived a fairytale life and our troubles no longer existed. There were many days I questioned myself, "Who am I?" My life was all over the place, filled with confusion and lies. In many cases, individuals refuse to admit this kind of life keeps you in turmoil, changing by the hour. Many times we cannot even recognize the fact that this problem is even a problem.

There comes a time when you must stop, evaluate your behaviors and review the company you keep. Some individuals partake in the behaviors presented and never realize the influence others have over our actions. Many times, we think we are leading our lives - when in reality, our surroundings are what influences our response to various situations.

I know reading this will make many individuals say "This chick is crazy", but pay close attention to your behaviors. You may possibly realize these things are happening without your knowledge because they have become part of your persona. I began noticing how I reacted to situations according to the mask I wore. To sum it up, we adapt to our environment. Fighters will become better fighters, hustlers become better hustlers and teachers become better teachers; we are what we invest time into becoming.

What we must realize is how our past can shape the

future masks we wear. In life, individuals learn to cover the things which shame us. Whether as a child or as an adult, when life presents situations that are displeasing, embarrassing, shameful and even traumatic - our subconscious mind begins to guard us from potentially harmful events.

A protective layer forms over our hearts, making us seem hard and cold on the outside to those who may invade these sensitive areas in life. To initiate the process of uncovering self-identity, one must remove each mask - one by one and face the issues that caused the hiding in the first place. It is difficult to be exposed to painful experiences which have taken control over one's life, but this is where the realization starts. Keeping these emotions suppressed will only hinder your growth process.

Identification is the beginning of the end. Identifying and addressing haunting issues releases the traumatic power it has over our life. Only then can you lay each mask down, tap into your inner soul and discover a sense of your true identity. Take the first step of the healing process and confess the issues you have been holding inside. Release those demons and free the inner potential of self-identity.

Who am I

Who am I, I scream and cry, who am I

As I watch unpleasing actions pass me by.

Who am I, no one can identify,

Who am I, living like scum

Who am I, just another street bum.

Who am I, living in fear?

Who am I looking for, any man who cares

Who am I, as I lay in the dark bed filled with tears.

Who am I, wishing someone could hear

Who am I, as I pray to God my fears

Who am I, slowing losing my pride

Who am I, someone help me please

Who am I, as I watch my vagina bleed? Who am I, God only knows

Who am I, I have nowhere else to go.

Who am I, as I wash my body with disgrace and shame?

Who am I, no one knows my pain. Who am I, I SCREAM AND CRY,

who am I, as I watch my SPIRIT DIE. Who am I, as I unmask my blame, who am I, another child of God

Living in shame

The mask represents events which have hurt us in life; unpleasant things we live with, such as our 'dirty little secrets' or just a little more 'stuff'. As we go through life carrying painful burdens, they will become too much to tolerate. These are the life-altering events we must face in order to move forward in the healing process. Believe me when I say the road becomes easier to travel when you lighten your load.

Many individuals commit suicide, live a life of crime or victimize others to escape pain; never realizing we hold the key to our own happiness by releasing negativity and regaining the power taken from us. No longer will we allow others to hurt us, nor will we continue to hurt ourselves with destructive behaviors and relationships. It's time to take back the power and glory because it is yours - it belongs to you. We will be victims no more. Living the life of a victim causes more pain and suffering, which in return allows dwelling in self-pity; self-pity leads to depression.

In summary, chapter two advises you to identify with who you are. It's time to pay close attention to your behaviors, your environment; how your behaviors change according to situations and the company you keep. I, along with many people lived a lie; full of shame and hurtful experiences that we concealed. Today, make a promise moving forward to practice self-identification. Take time to learn who you are, what you like and create a true connection within you.

When you begin this process each day, you build a deeper relationship with self as the masks are slowly removed. By learning to control your inner feelings, you may find yourself in more control of your moods and create a happier space within.

Reflections for the Soul

After reading chapter 2 'The Mask', allow yourself time to think and process the information as it relates to your life. Think about the person you represent for the world to see and be honest about identifying your areas of truth that need growth. Self-identity is a major component in the growth process of life; use your mirror to view the key elements keeping you in bondage.

As you reflect on your image, take notes and challenge yourself to work through self-improvement to rebuild the person within. Review the starter questions, begin the healing and connect with your mirror image of self-identity and begin removing you're mask.

Reflection Questions

1 List the people who create mood-altering situations for you.

2. Ask yourself why you feel the need to mask who you are?

3. What type of mask are you wearing? Identify what you feel.

4. For each mask, ask yourself "Do I want to continue giving this person the power to keep me in bondage?"

5. Now ask yourself the most important question; are you willing and ready to take control of your feelings starting today?

CHAPTER III

DEPRESSION

As I lay in my bed, just staring at the ceiling, wondering who is this person I have grown to be, the sadness that lives inside of me as I hide a heart of stone, left with no pride only lost dreams and rage that I hold inside. Only my stained pillow will know all the tears I've cried, lost is a world living in fear, I regret the evenings as darkness appears. My soul has cried because night is here as I lay in the bed praying to God that somehow my father could hear or hold me just once and whisper soft words with a gentle touch, but there is no father only the man who wants to be called daddy as he slowly removes my little panties, he climbs on top and moans, as I lay and pray Lord this cannot be; my heart goes cold as each part of my soul, is slowly removed and my body grows old, soon I have no feeling I no longer can care, my innocence is taken I'm left confused gasping for air, now my life is different for beauty I no longer can see, as depression quickly consumes me, my eyes are now dark and cold, my flowers become black as mold as I hate the skin that I now live in, I reach up to heaven and ask Lord why me, with tears in my eyes I look at my veins wondering if I slice them will it stop the pain, I open my mouth to scream but there is no sound only distant cars that I hear from a far while he tastes my juices and indulges my treasures not understanding these moans are not sounds of pleasures, what happened to the child that lived in me who was covered with blood sweat and depression yes that's me, you see he took something special on that night he murdered me, now I live a dark gloom and I just don't care for I'm SO tired of changing soiled underwear, where is my father the man who loves and protects me, where is my father to teach me how to love with a kind gentle touch, you know the father who is supposed to love me so much, How do I begin to right this wrong when I look for a father who was always gone. Now I know I can't change what has already happened to me but I need you fathers to stop and see; that little girl so innocent sweet as can be; stop leaving her alone to run these streets we need you more than words can ever explain cause other men will only cause us pain only you can protect our hearts and fathers we need this from the very start show us love and always be there for that other man may keep us living in shame and fear so I scream out loud and please take heed because I was a victim yes a victim you see another fatherless child yes that was me. So for years I walked in depression and shame while my father ran the streets and put dope in his veins. Now trust and believe I will blame my mother too because she choose that glass pipe to mask the pain over you as she chased her cloud she left me free at the hands of this man and she could not see how my innocence was being taken again and again by this man she had me calling let's just say Uncle Ben, See this depression was real for me as well you, because I wanted to get high to feel like you do; no throbbing no hurt just numb and dark, masking my pain from the very start when I had my children and suddenly looked to see the depression had to stop because it was killing me I fell to my knees and began to pray Lord please stop this depression please take the pain away No longer do I blame my parents for my life I have hired a new pilot and now we take flight His name is Jesus He is now in control this depression is gone, He has soothed my soul, the love I thought I needed from you has been provided you see,

The dark curse you gave has been broken for me

Dear God I thank you because now I am FREE.

Depression can live within individuals for years and may rob us of our happiness and success. For several years, I lived in agony and self-pity, which quickly lead to my life of self-destruction. These vicious cycles are patterns of hurt traveling from generation to generation because the pain prevents us from providing the love and support our children need in order to become productive individuals in society.

Somehow, the traumatic events which have occurred in our lives cause us to inflict more pain upon ourselves and others. We in return, hate ourselves because of the situations experienced by the hands of another. As we mask the hurt and shame, it slowly devours the beautiful person living within us and we shield ourselves in a depressive state of mind, unaware of the circumstances.

My body was accustomed to being hurt, so pain was the only thing I knew. Therefore, drugs, alcohol and promiscuous behaviors came natural for me; those were the self-destructive traits that I was taught by my abusers. Although this was the life I lived, it was not very pleasing on the inside and caused conflicting battles within me. It is an example of how an individual wants something different, yet has no clue how to change. These depressive behaviors made many situations difficult to deal with. I always find myself reflecting on the cartoon *Tom and Jerry,* where the angel and devil are sitting on their shoulders giving them the option of doing good or bad things. Well, everyone experiences having to make choices in life.

When an individual suffers from depression, their perception of right and wrong is controlled by circumstances. I say this because God always shows us the way and provides an escape. Most often we fail to listen to our inner feelings and the deeper we fall into depression, the more our choices are clouded. This allows us an opportunity to hurt ourselves and slowly, we lose sight of the fact that we've become our own abusers. As children, we never really understand how our young minds are manipulated by our abusers. Please understand that abuse comes in many forms; mental, sexual and physical, which kills the creativity of young minds and causes major internal conflicts.

Depression reveals itself in various forms depending on the individual and the trauma which initiated the depressive state of mind. I was lucky to have a childhood friend who noticed I was in a severe depression. I remember my situation as if it happened yesterday. At this lowest point in my life; my children were in elementary school, I was not working and I was alone - juggling three to four relationships with various men who supplied my different needs. I drank alcohol every day and had a horrible marijuana addiction, which caused me to have a miscarriage. I had just broken up with who I thought was the love of my life (another drug dealer) who supplied my habits.

To make matters worse, my sister had moved back to Sulfur, Virginia to continue her college education. Now because I claim to be a strong individual, there was no way in the world I could allow my sister to know the pain I really felt by her leaving - but deep down inside, a part of me died the day my sister and I parted. Please understand my relationship with my sister is very unique only because we are not biological sisters; God placed us together and we were inseparable.

My sister is very smart, so pursuing college is

something I had to encourage and not dare think of my own selfish reasons for needing her to stay. However, the feelings of abandonment overwhelmed my heart once again because I thought I was losing the only person who cared about my well-being. Yes I still had my brothers and my daughters, but they needed me to be the strong leader and mother – even though I relied on my sister for strength, wisdom, support, guidance and courage because she believed my life would change. Her feelings were genuine and pure. So with the unselfish love I have for my sister, I wished her well on her journey to better herself while I struggled in silence.

With my sister, I was never alone - nor was I judged for my actions, so I needed her to know I would be ok. This is where my life spiraled totally out of control and self-destruction was all I could see in my future. Drugs, sex and money were all my life needed and in between the lonely days; I stayed locked in my room, sheltered from the outside world and drowning in misery. I have heard the saying "When one door closes, God opens another", but I never understood what that meant until now.

After my sister left and I thought I was alone, a childhood friend was the Angel God placed before me to save my life. He visited me every day and I never understood why. Early in the morning, he was at my house and stayed until the wee hours of the night. With him being at the house, I had to cook and make sure my girls got off to school on time - then back in the bed I went, while he sat and played video games as I slept away my sorrows. Occasionally he would wake me - I guess to make sure I was not dead, or to drink those nasty ensure drinks he brought me every day because I would not eat (depression will steal your appetite). Nevertheless, he was there every day and to this day, I do not know why.

Then one day he looked at me and said, "Pooh you are suffering from depression" and I just laughed. He told me there was a commercial on television and I needed to pay attention to the symptoms, because I needed help - if not for me, then for my daughters. Wow, my daughters… at that moment I realized my depression did in fact affect my children, so I watched the commercial. To my surprise, I had all the symptoms. Suicide was at the bottom of the list and although I thought of killing myself on many occasions - knowing the pain it would bring my children, I did not entertain that thought much. Killing myself was not an option not for me. For my daughters I had to live; I loved them too much to cause their lives pain because I decided to quit.

Listen, depression is real and some people never recover. I realized I did not want to die. As I started looking in the mirror daily, I had to be completely honest with myself and address the issues which were slowly killing me from the inside out. I began to admit that what I felt was hurt, pain and shame. I was lonely, scared, consumed with anger, hatred, disappointment and a host of other things. Many people get stuck at this point. We move through life trying to cover and hide the hurt we feel.

Our mental state suffers and we 'act out' opposed to addressing the real issues. Most of these behaviors are very self-destructive; some develop bad eating habits, sexual addictions, as well as drug addiction - anything to mask the pain of depression. Suddenly, life becomes a task too big to endure and it's almost impossible to find one positive thing to hold on to.

Through the pain, I had to find a reason to get free and continue life; my children became my reason to live. You must find your reason to keep going on in life. As I stood in the mirror, I asked God "How do I begin to change?" "How do I make it better?" Each day I cried to myself and my vision began to clear. I was able to accept some of my abandonment issues, because life had to go on and it was time for me to take control of who I was and what I wanted in this world.

I had to realize not everyone is put in our life to stay forever - sometimes it is just for a purpose. His purpose was to help me see my horrible state of depression and find my way back to living life. My childhood friend was there as a filler. He was in my life for a reason and was the vessel God sent to protect me from myself and when his purpose was served, he moved on to his next mission in life. Finally, the doors of acceptance were opened and my journey out of depression began. I cannot thank him enough. He may not even know or understand how much his presence was needed, but with all my heart I will never forget the vital role he played in saving my life. Thank you my friend.

In summary, chapter three exposes the silent killer of many young people - depression. Individuals are suffering in a quiet world of pain and hurt, living with this disease that causes so many problems in many areas. People often live a life that is full of pain, disappointment and fear. Today, make a promise moving forward to seek help. When you seek help by talking to someone, surround yourself with positive energy. Get help - never try to handle depression alone. Life gets better when you view it through a different lens. Don't let the silent killer of depression take over your life and keep you hostage. Start talking to someone today - you will be thankful tomorrow.

Reflections for the Soul

After reading chapter Three, Depression; realize you should start talking and surrounding yourself with positive energy. You must take time to think and process what you feel as it relates to your life. Think about the things you may need to discuss in order to release the hurt; let go of the pain, seek counseling and just start talking - don't hold that pain any longer. Be honest about self-destructive behaviors so you can address your needs for growth.

As you reflect on the depressing areas of your life, take notes and challenge yourself to talk about these situations. Start working out these areas - as this will help reinforce your self-esteem and rebuild the person within. I have listed starter questions for you to begin the healing process and generate useful, healing conversations.

Reflection Questions

1. Are you suffering from depression?
2. Identify the behaviors associated with depression.
3. Do you have immediate resources for communication?
4. Do you have feelings of hurting yourself or others?
5. Promise to talk to someone - and if you do not have someone available, you will reach out to a crisis hotline for professional help!

***The crisis hotline is available 24 hours a day, 7 days a week: 1-855-401-2484**

LAVETTE WILLIS-CRITTENTON

CHAPTER IV
ACCEPTANCE

A still moment in time, I sit and pray to be free,

A still moment in time to evaluate me,

I must face the hurt and embrace the shame or forever I'll live in dyer pain

I shall face my enemies and hold them to blame

This battle is not over nor have you won this game.

I will fight 'til the end until victory I declare,

As I slay your heart with the sharpest sphere.

The smell of death now fills the atmosphere, as you gasp for air;

In me is life I can surely breathe,

Because finally I've done just one good deed.

As you look upon me with tears in your eyes,

Slowly I feel me regaining my pride,

The life you stole no longer you keep, Accept what you've done, Accept this DEFEAT.

When it is time for individuals to face acceptance, flashbacks of life cross the mind. We view our life and finally see how much pain, guilt, anger - and most of all depression, contributed to the harmful life we live. Acceptance makes a situation come to life because you have to admit 'yes this happened to me', now what? When facing acceptance, consider what happened to you or the pain you inflicted upon someone else. This becomes yet another vital point in your therapeutic process for the next phase of healing.

Let me interpret my analysis of how acceptance was perceived in my eyes as a victim - then I will share my perception as the abuser. In my younger years, I experienced many days not understanding why my life was in such disarray; living in constant fear of what could be.

Not knowing when or where the next meal would come from, for a child - this was daunting. I lived a life of crime as a means of survival because that is the only answer offered on the streets. Then you have sexual abuse inflicted upon you by many men who take advantage of their chance to gain sexual satisfaction from wounded victims, just because opportunity presents itself. It creates a horrible self-image, while adding to the mental abuse that follows and haunts your life in the process. At this point, I chose to fault everyone for the hurt I suffered as a child.

I blamed my mother and father for being addicts and for not being the parents I needed to guide and raise me. I blamed my grandparents, aunts and uncles; I even blamed God. *I blamed everyone for my anguish because I was the victim. I needed someone and no one was there; a young child suffering with no help - only tears of fear and pain. Generating a build-up of negative energy from years of turmoil; well it must be released eventually - that is when anger begins to show in our behaviors. These behaviors represent the victim's cry for help that adults fail to notice or recognize.*

VICTIMS

I once was a victim, broken battered and abused you see

I once was a victim hiding my scares, so no one can see

I once was a victim alone in this world

I once was a victim a lost little girl

I once was a victim and you took advantage of me

I once was a victim and you could not see

I once was a victim and I hated me

I once was a victim who prayed to be free

I once was a victim who dreamed my last breath

I once was a victim who had nothing left

I once was a victim who became hard as stone

I once was a victim who was all alone

Alone was I in this world just me

A victim no more, I will not be

This anger and pain I give back to thee

A victim no more, I will not BE.

No longer being a victim quickly led to my becoming a victimizer. Once my heart filled with angry force, the only thing I could do was release it somehow. It resulted in disruptive behaviors which not only harmed others, but me as well. These disruptive behaviors enabled me to put others in the 'victim's seat' because I no longer wanted to be a victim; it was about the survival game - get them before they get you. This was the method to my madness. I was bound for self-destruction. My target was men; I hurt every man I encountered and had no respect for any elder who dared to complain or question my actions. This became my way of life; my perception of the world grew cold and heartless. That's what I gave because it was all I was taught in life.

One day something came over me and suddenly - I wanted my power back. My heart screamed ENOUGH! I cried, blamed everyone I could think of and then I cried some more, until finally I was all cried out and wanted answers. I wanted to end the curse that was shamed upon my family and break the vicious cycle. I wanted something different for my children. I wanted my children to have happy memories, but those were something I could not identify with. I began to pray, but this time it was different because I no longer wanted to pray for sympathy. I just wanted peace; peace to deal with the stressful life I was living.

Every night I sat listening to gospel music in my living room and suddenly I could feel God touching my soul. For the first time in my life I held myself with all my might, tears streaming down my face; I prayed and prayed for understanding and finally, GOD answered. He touched my heart and said ACCEPTANCE.

I finally accepted all that had happened in my life and focused on my favorite saying, "You will get over it."

I gave the hurt and pain to the individuals who deserved it because they were no longer my burdens. Finally, I realized acceptance is about owning the mistakes we make in life and holding others accountable for their actions.

Acceptance is not easy because when individuals look at the role they play in various situations, folks must accept the fact that mistakes were made. Something went wrong. What did I do? Where did I go wrong? This phase of the healing process forces individuals to take responsibility for all the right and wrong committed in life.

Whether you have committed wrong against others or someone has committed wrong against you - look at each situation for what it is and respond accordingly. In the event someone has wronged you, now is the time to return it to its rightful owner. Never will I tell anyone to carry the responsibility of someone else's burdens - you have done this for far too long.

If someone has hurt you in anyway, now is the time to face it and accept that it happened. This is not your fault; it is someone else's wrong- doing which must be made right. However, if you plan to move forward - confront the problem and address it. Address the hurt and pain you carry in your heart and let your abuser carry the burden the rest of the way. Only then can you accept the behaviors you display. Only then will you understand why you choose to harm or cause pain to yourself and others.

Without acceptance and acknowledgement we tend to keep issues buried deep inside us, pretending they never occurred and just like old meat, it begins to rot. Sometimes we need to face our accusers and express our hurt or pain. In some cases this may not be possible, or may result in additional frustration for you. Understand that acceptance might be as simple as making peace within yourself, knowing what happened to you is truly not your fault. Acceptance is no longer blaming or pointing fingers at your abuser because that keeps you in bondage. I realized I must give it back to that sick individual; this is when the heart opens up for healing. Then and only then, was I able to forgive.

In summary, my hope for you in Chapter four, Acceptance is for you to pinpoint your own problems. Acceptance is not about blame – it's about understanding someone hurt you and that you must let it go to move forward. People - including myself, have blamed ourselves for the pain others caused. No, this is not what I need for you here; you have been living a life with stolen dreams, because someone stole your joy.

Today, make a promise moving forward to give the hurt back to its rightful owner. You cannot change what happened, however you can control your future. When you accept this and return it to its owner, it releases you from being held hostage. Make sure you control your future and begin to heal from now on.

Reflections for the Soul

After reading Chapter Four - Acceptance, allow time to think and process the information as it relates to your life. Think about the person you represent to the world and be honest about what you are accepting for growth. Once we reach the conclusion that someone hurt us and we are not responsible for their actions, we gain control of our actions today. A major component in the growth process is the ability to understand; understanding areas we can and cannot change to avoid confusion and being stifled. As you reflect on the areas of acceptance in your inner conflicts, take notes and challenge yourself to work through self-improvement and restore the person within. I have listed starter questions that will assist you with accepting the pain for release and start healing from within.

Reflection Questions

1. What are some challenges you need to accept?

2. Do you believe acceptance is part of your healing process?

3. Are you ready to begin the healing process and release yourself?

4. Make a promise that no longer will you allow someone to keep you in bondage and control your emotions.

5. Are you willing to wake up each day and take ownership of your happiness?

LAVETTE WILLIS-CRITTENTON

CHAPTER V

FORGIVENESS

Forgiving my enemies, for the pain they have caused me;

Running from my shadows of these scars that marks me

No more space in my heart for sorrow to crowd me

Praying for a way to forgive you for these sins

In search of a way for my healing to begin

Removing the bondage that has me dying within

The pain I carry, you may never know

But forgiving you allows me to let it go

Forgiving those who have wounded me,

for it has kept me hostage and I need to be free

The hurt and anger I hold within, forgiving you will release that sin;

It has taken a while just to understand,

the power of forgiving removes your hands

I no longer want my life to remain a reflection of you,

This cycle must end our relationship is through;

The power you stole belongs to me; my heart must heal I need to be free

So as I leave; because yes, I must go;

I learned in life, you reap just what you sow.

Today I stand a changed person, proud as can be because forgiving you

Is what released ME

Forgiving people has been by far the hardest part of my healing process. For years, I struggled with forgiving people who caused harm to my life. What I realized over time is that I remained in bondage; stuck in self-pity regarding the events of my past and therefore, my life could not move past the focus of hurt. Each day I re-lived the experience in my mind, which in return affected every relationship I tried to build. This habit enabled me to build a wall of resistance and shelter my true feelings to avoid areas where I felt most vulnerable.

With no effort at all, I somehow found ways to sabotage any relationship that came close to gaining space in my heart. My entire life was based around abandonment issues from my childhood.

I moved forward in life expecting people to eventually leave me, so all my relationships were viewed as short term. This attitude justified the wrongful actions and behaviors I displayed. I never understood how much of my life was impacted by fear of abandonment.

The importance of understanding why we need to forgive is an adventurous learning process. Allow me to elaborate just a bit, starting with my parents. Having an absent parent is a vastly common issue people struggle with for years; let's explore the absent father.

Be reminded this is only *my* perspective on the subject. I noticed that not having a father around prevented me from learning what a man's role in my life was supposed to be. I never experienced the comfort, protection and support a father provides when he is in the home or just a part of a child's life.

Our fathers are there to show how a man should love us. He protects and provides a level of trust which permits a child to feel safe – therefore, we discover what to look for as we grow and develop relationships in our adult life. When this part of our life is not nurtured, we search for all the wrong qualities in the men we have intimate relationships with. We tend to seek a 'father figure' in our personal life, which can be a burden to your mate. We never learn how it feels to be in a safe, loving space with the gentle, unconditional affection that only a father can give his daughter. Our boys suffer because the skills they need to develop into positive, strong men were never instilled.

The result is that our boys have no idea what manhood is about. Our boys have no clue regarding what the duties of a man entail. They never learned how to please and protect a woman or just support a home, because they have not been taught. We live our lives by the actions and morals we were taught as children.

Fathers have roles and duties in their children's lives for reasons; to groom boys to be men and to shield girls as they become trusting, submissive women.

When our mothers are the absent parent, the family suffers the same way. Our children lack the nurturing comfort which only a mother can provide. She teaches young girls grooming skills; how to love herself, respect herself and how to cater to the home. Our mothers are supposed to provide life skills which enhance a young girl's motherly instincts.

There are some who assume this type of self-development comes naturally – NO, someone must illustrate these things within the home. For our boys - a mother demonstrates love, support and comfort. A mother feeds and aids boys, grooming their minds into a happy space. Over the years, I realized GOD made man and woman for a reason; we each have unique roles in life and are equally important in raising children to be productive individuals. Therefore, when one or both parents are absent from a child's life it becomes a recipe for disaster. At no fault of your own and as a product of your situation - YOU must learn to get over it. In a perfect world, we want our parents to protect us, comfort us, shield us and love us 'blah blah blah' - yeah so did I. Nevertheless, ask yourself this "Do I remain stuck because of what my parents did not do?" NO!

I realize they were never able to heal their own hurts and in return, I paid the price - however, I will not make my children suffer from my pain, so therefore I must heal. Healing begins the change and change begins the healing.

In summary, I hope chapter five encourages forgiveness. In order to identify with who you are and move past the hurt, you must forgive those who've caused you pain. When people go through life with an unforgiving heart, it hinders the growth process. Today, make a promise moving forward to forgive.

When you look in the mirror, tell yourself exactly how you feel about the situation and start the healing by forgiving; you are forever held hostage until you do. Today I forgive - not for you, but for me because I need to move past this stage of my life and get closer to my true self.

Reflections for the Soul

After reading Chapter five - Forgiveness; take time to process the information as it pertains to your life and the individuals you need to forgive. Think about the person and understand that this is for you - not them, because there will be times when you'll question why you are forgiving that horrible person. Be really honest about wanting to grow in your life. Forgiveness is a major component for growth in life. Use your mirror to view your soul and see the key elements keeping you in bondage.

As you reflect on your image, take notes and challenge yourself to work through self-improvement and rebuild the person within. I have listed a few starter questions to begin the healing process of connecting with the mirror image of forgiveness.

Reflection Questions

1. Do you believe that forgiving your accusers is for your personal growth?

2. Have you reached a point in your life where you're ready to forgive the people who hurt you?

3. List the people you believe you need to forgive.

4. Write your forgiveness statement; explain who, what and why you have chosen to forgive each individual.

5. Read your forgiveness statement each day until you can wholeheartedly forgive them.

CHAPTER VI

CHANGE

The progression of change is something I have battled with throughout my life. I have always challenged myself to do better because I probably will always see myself as an under-privileged child living in a crack house. Those memories are haunting and give me distorted thinking patterns. Today, I see how my behaviors have changed over the years. In my heart, I never wanted to be like my mother; a woman I saw as an addict, weakened from abusive men and defeated by life. Therefore, I tried everything in my power to be the opposite of what I saw in my mother – not realizing I was running in the same path of destruction.

The life I saw as a child was all I knew and it followed me every day; no matter where I went, those nasty old habits were right behind me. I started dating local drug dealers because they gave me money and drugs and in exchange, I gave myself; this was the beginning of my self-inflicted abuse pattern. Abusing my body was how I started supporting my brothers, my children and myself - no more hungry nights. I was a teen mother and high school drop-out with a bad marijuana habit - so the life that was already rough, just got rougher. All the bills and maintaining a household, quickly became overwhelming and a major source of stress.

With nowhere to turn or look for help, I searched for ways to escape the mess of a life I was living. I was never taught how to cope with stress, therefore life was getting the best of me. Using drugs, drinking and abusing my body became my way of coping with the everyday stressors of life. I had no clue I was losing the battle. I was fifteen with two children and my two brothers, who became my responsibility.

Determined not to be like my mother, I hustled to make ends meet and keep the bills paid. I was now able to dress up in fancy clothes with lipstick and high heels, pretending to be an adult. I was handling my business - I mean really holding us down. I was not on crack, my family was not hungry and we all had plenty of clothes to wear now. We went from rags to riches. Yes, I drank and smoked a little weed - even went out partying, but I made sure my family was okay. In my eyes, I was perfect just the way I was. However when I was alone, I had to admit all the flaws in my reflection. Deep down inside I hated the person staring back at me, because I saw who I was trying so hard not to be - my mother.

One day, while staring at the mirror my mind traveled back in time; I suddenly saw my life flash before me and there I was once again, that scared little girl. I had to be about ten years old when I first recognized I was born into a dysfunctional family.

I noticed how my attitude towards my living arrangements seemed to display embarrassment, opposed to accepting them as normal. Living in a dark, dingy house with constant sounds of doors opening and closing day and night from a high-traffic crack house; empty cabinets, no hot water and hot plates, somehow no longer felt right. My life was now a terrible experience of shame and humiliation. The life I was in was not my own.

Flashbacks of my childhood haunt me to this day. Fear of never having enough food or utilities being shut off for non-payment; even having an over-crowded home, sends my mind into a spinning rage and it took years for me to make the connection back to my childhood experiences. That is when I realized I was putting my children through those same situations. No I was not on crack; I had a different drug of choice, but I was still on the verge of becoming an addict. At that moment I realized I needed to change, if not for me - for my children.

Once I was able to see my life following the patterns established by my family history, I could change the pathway. I was then capable of choosing another route or continuing down the same path my mother chose; a path of drugs, parties, sex and men. I looked at my daughters and realized I didn't want them to see me the way I saw my mother. I knew I needed to make a change in my life somehow; I needed to break the cycle of high school drop-outs, teen pregnancies and drug addiction.

I wanted more for my daughters - but how do I begin to show them something I have yet to learn myself, was the question? How could I force education onto these two, innocent, little girls when I did not practice what I was preaching to them? I needed to change. I needed my daughters to see me differently. I wanted them to be proud to say I was their mother. I wanted to give them a better life. I needed to change!

At that moment I felt my eyes filling with tears because I was failing my daughters. I wanted something different for my daughters - yet I had no clue how to get it, so I started with the smallest choice (which was the biggest of them all); I stopped using and selling drugs. It was not easy. My body went through all types of withdrawal symptoms, but I needed to focus.

Slowly, things started looking differently viewing them through sober eyes. My picture of life looked different. I could no longer stand the mess in the house, so I cleaned up and it felt better living in a clean house. No more drug use, meant no more friends selling drugs, which meant I had less money. This encouraged me to get a job. Some of the small changes made a huge difference in my life. Just having the ability to view my life with sober eyes allowed me to see areas of self-improvement.

These were much needed changes and had nothing to do with my surroundings or lifestyle, but everything to do with me. I began to work on me. What I learned is that when you make the decision to change *you*; no doubt, your surroundings and lifestyle will automatically change. I stopped feeling sorry for the hand I was dealt in life and started playing it. Changing myself allowed me to get into the game of life. Making positive changes helped me realize how long I felt sorry for myself and this kept me pitiful and stuck in my mess.

I did not have any mentors or role models to lead the way however, I had the Cosby show. Some might laugh when they read this statement, but it became the guiding point in my direction towards change. The one person I truly admired was Phyllicia Rashad. In my mind she was perfect in every way. I do not know Phyllicia Rashad personally - yet the role she played as Clair Huxtable was the picture of perfection I still see in her today. She exhibited the guiding principles of womanhood and somehow I wanted to mimic her life. I found someone to take me from who I was, to who I wanted to become.

This ignited my voyage of changing my attitude, my behaviors, my thoughts, my desires, my needs, my values, my mind, my friends, my actions and my life. I changed me. I saw myself in a dream and I wanted that Cosby show lifestyle.

I wanted to be that beautiful black woman; 'educated, respected, cherished by her husband and children' type of woman. I wanted that for me.

These daydreams gave me hope and something to aim for in life however - I didn't have a road map for achieving these dreams. So now, the seed was planted in my mind with no clue how to nurture its transformation. One day I sat and wrote all the things I liked about myself and all the things I disliked about myself; somehow seeing these things in writing made it clear where I needed to start. Once I saw the information on paper, I was able to correct each issue one task at a time.

I had to be completely honest when doing my self-evaluation and some major issues were revealed. I discovered key issues which really affected my self-esteem. Now please realize this area will be different for everyone. You must express your true feelings; you will not be able to fix problems in your life if you don't admit there is need for repair. Here are a few of my secrets that kept me in bondage: I never viewed myself as being smart because I dropped out of high school. I had a mean spirit filled with anger, so I could not love. I never completed projects I started due to a fear of failure; it was easier to just quit. I was a slave to money; I was always broke and without any savings because I shopped with every penny trying to buy my happiness. I was not good enough for any man to love, so I never wanted a relationship; I thought 'who could love a person like me?' I had no hair due to stress, perms and weaves which affected my looks and damaged my self-esteem.

My attitude was a stinking mess because I didn't respect anyone or anything. My choice of words displayed my limited vocabulary. I dressed like a slut because I only had my body to offer, so it was always on display. I had no love for who I was, unwanted and unloved as a child. I could go on forever but these are just a few of my issues that needed to be addressed when I saw a desire for personal change. It was very hurtful to look at myself and my heart - such 'stinking thinking', but this was how I saw myself.

This attitude was how I displayed myself to the world. People only see what we show them and if this is how I saw my life, I could only receive what I put out. I reviewed the list of ugliness in my life and trust me, the list was quite long. I started making promises to myself. My first promise was to finish whatever I start; I don't care how long it takes to complete and no matter the outcome - good or bad, my job is to reach the finish line. With that being said, I had to complete my first project in life; earning my high school diploma. My life could go no further without completing that one little piece of the puzzle. It really is our first accomplishment in life and sets the foundation for our future.

Again fear knocked at my door, but this time I was stronger. Since I was no longer high or drunk, I could see it knocking and yelling "No Dummy No!" I could not be defeated before I got started, so I kept my thoughts to myself. One Saturday morning I went to Temple and applied to take the GED exam. All types of fears ran through my head and to make matters worse, everyone waiting to take the exam had nothing but negative comments adding to my anxiety. I just sat quietly in a corner on the floor as I awaited the exam, praying for God to let me do my best and stay positive.

I had to return on three different occasions to complete the entire exam. Afraid to open my results for fear of being disappointed; I waited until all the exams were completed, then opened the final results which changed my life. I faced one of my toughest fears and it opened doors I never imagined. For the first time in my life, I was so proud of myself! I had something positive to share and began seeing myself in a new light. I was smarter than I gave myself credit for and it sparked a new feeling inside. I believe in myself – wow, what an experience this created. A small internal change armed me with the courage to face a fear which kept me defeated. I was now introduced to a feeling of loving who I am.

Change

A change in my heart, is like a planted seed

With love and nurture the growth begins

A change in my heart, creates a new breed

Replacing damaging events with positive future plans

With smiles and feelings of I think I can

Small changes in life is all one needs

To begin to add life to a dying breed

Just helping one individual see the need for change

Will enhance a generation left with no plan just pain

A change in my heart forms a new start

A change in my mind slowly changed time

And soon I was able to see

Small changes in life were helping me

See all the love I thought was missing

I found in me

These changes started just in my mind

Somehow exposed what I needed to see

To begin a changed life of loving me!

In summary, the purpose of Chapter Six - Change; is to help you identify who you are. Today, make a promise to be the person you envision yourself as. When you look in the mirror, tell yourself exactly who you are or you will never see a need to change. Fear and pain can make us ugly, however - today the wounds can heal by speaking the truth about your real personality. Accept the fact that you are a renewed person and live everyday as the person you always dreamed of being.

Reflections for the Soul

When you've finished reading this chapter, think about the message and how it pertains to you. Think about the perception you give to the world and identify the parts of your personality requiring growth. As you reflect on your image, commit to using self-improvement techniques to rebuild your core. Use these questions to start the healing process, because change begins with you.

Reflection Questions

1. Are you ready to commit to making a change for yourself?

2. Are you willing to ignore those who will challenge your change process?

3. List the individuals who will serve as your silent sources of inspiration. This could be your children, parents, husband or anyone who will provide you with strength when you feel weak.

4. How do you see yourself? Write out your one, five and ten-year plans. This is your action plan for growth.

5. What is your process for achieving your plan? Do you want to go back to school? Do you need to save money? Focus on your goals and put your plan into action.

LAVETTE WILLIS-CRITTENTON

CHAPTER VII

LOVING YOURSELF

Loving yourself opens a whole new world of experiences. It is a new adventure and something I had to learn. Trust me it took some time - ok, *a whole lot of time*. When we go through life feeling unloved and unwanted, we grow accustomed to that empty feeling and don't even recognize that we haven't learned to love ourselves due to the emptiness. It is hard to recognize behaviors that are harmful and damaging because it's all we know.

As we hurt others with our negative attitude and actions, it infects our hearts and turns them to stone. This creates a nasty image and determines how we address issues and individuals throughout our lives. Please keep in mind that it takes years of hurt and pain for someone's heart to turn to stone and it will take just as long - if not longer, to heal the wounds. What I realized is that the more I faced my demons - the stronger I became. Yes, you read that right - I said demons!

These are the demons in our head and hearts that keep us confined to self-hatred. They keep us in abusive relationships and self-destructive behaviors. They make us rely on someone else's energy. Learning to love yourself is part of the path to true happiness and unlocks things you never knew existed.

Learning to love yourself is taking time to inspect your heart's desires for things, such as what inspires you; what dreams are lurking in your mind and what types of activities you enjoy. When we take this time to entertain ourselves, we discover what we like and what we want out of life. Making time to spend quality time alone is how one can find the answers to true happiness.

At one point in my life, I felt like my daughters were my happiness and my means for living. I found strength in their existence. Yeah, I know it sounds sad - yet having my children was the blessing God knew I would need in life. Remember, I had children and was responsible for my brothers at a very early age, so my childhood was short-lived and then I got married. Most of my life was spent nurturing someone; I never had time to really get to know myself.

I moved through life fulfilling dreams, traveling the world with my spouse and transitioning my children into adulthood. I believed I was living the American dream; you know my 'Cosby show' lifestyle. However, as my children became more independent - I started feeling worthless, harboring feelings of abandonment once again. My babies were doing what I raised them to do; work and being responsible. My daughters were becoming young women; working and dating was their daily routine.

My daughters were responsible, they even cooked for themselves - which made me feel like they no longer needed me to be mommy. This made me stop and correct my 'stinking thinking' to say, "NO your babies love you and they are doing just what you taught them." So why did I feel empty? One day I came home from work, looked around the house and no one was there but me. I was stronger and smarter this time, so I asked myself a specific question, "What would you like to do now that you have free time?" Guess what - I had no idea.

I was clueless as to what I even enjoyed because it was never about me; always my children and their needs, my spouse and his needs. So I began searching for my happiness. I started surfing the internet and decided to go back to school to pursue a degree. School provided no time for a pity party. I had plenty of school work to keep me focused and busy. I had somewhere to go, meeting new people - while building myself esteem at the same time. As I progressed further into my dream of having a degree, I could see the life I used to dream for myself.

I discovered just how important it is to achieve goals, dreams and milestones in life because they are foundational pieces of you. My Saturday mornings were no longer dedicated to making breakfast or housework.

I was up early going to the coffee shop just to sit, have coffee and study and I loved it. I explored new options of entertainment; going to plays, shopping for myself, going to the gym, relaxing on a sunny day or enjoying a good book. I even enjoyed attending church services. I was learning to spend time with me. Finally, I was enjoying the life I used to dream of living.

Each day we experience something different. It provides another opportunity to get life right. We will always have challenges - but we should learn from past mistakes, fears and experiences how to adjust and deal with each situation life presents. I'm not saying it will be easy because that is not realistic; there will always be issues and people will hurt us. The difference is that we can recognize what *is* our problem and what is *not* our problem as well. When we love ourselves, we develop a better understanding of what we need to create that happy space in our life. We depend on others less and less because we fill our own void.

As children, we depend on others for our needs and wants. When these basic needs are not met, this is internalized - creating feelings of sadness and set on 'repeat'. We replay these feelings in our childhood and as we grow older, we bring these unresolved issues into our adulthood and that feeling of dependency continues to linger. We think this is all life has to offer and it becomes a battle to be happy.

When we meet someone new, attention is given and it fills the void - but it never lasts long. Before you know it, we argue and fuss claiming, "They just don't make me happy anymore." Shame on me to depend on someone else for my happiness. Reality check; we have all been there at some point in time. Perhaps we buy something new and our adrenaline is pumping; we enjoy the feeling of being momentarily satisfied, but that too never lasts long. It's a vicious cycle of trying to find happiness in all the wrong ways.

Once we realize happiness starts within us, not the circumstances affecting us - we understand the responsibility belongs to the individual. I am not saying we don't need people, things or money; we will always need these things, but they will never satisfy your problems regarding happiness. The more we focus on our higher power and achieving our dreams and goals in life, the more content we are with self-gratification. The empty holes in our life are slowly filled with pleasantries of self-satisfaction, which begins the process of being made 'whole' - being happy and loving who you are. You feel confident, strong and think on a new level. You take responsibility for your actions and admit your wrongs. You identify your true emotional state and finally take control of your emotions. If you don't learn to love yourself, it is almost impossible to give love to someone else.

Despite all this work and self-love, there will still be times when the same old demons will try to infect your thinking again and again. Therefore, always use these tips to remain focused; moving forward with new dreams and goals, constantly experiencing new feelings of satisfaction. Being in a better place emotionally and spiritually will automatically make you think differently. You are now responsible for your place in life; success or failure is your problem.

Always consider the following logic statements regarding your life: If I do not eat, it is because I did not cook. If I do not have food, it is because I did not go shopping. If I have no money, it is because I did not get a job. If I have bad credit, it is because I didn't pay my bills and if I don't have savings, it is because I didn't budget. So now, look in the mirror and ask yourself "Did I make me happy today?" The key word is I; I am the sole person responsible for me. I once suffered from abandonment, but when those old feelings trying to resurface - I must remember that is not my life today.

I have learned to love myself and I ensure that everyone I come in contact with respects my personal space, my time and my feelings. If something or someone hurts me intentionally or unintentionally, I express my feelings and decide how to address the relationship moving forward.

I am much more giving of myself now because my heart can receive affection from others, as well as give affection. I no longer need a man to make me feel whole, or provide my necessities because I am capable of doing it on my own. I make the choice of who stays in my life and why. I have finally reached a point where I can truly say I love the person I have become - flaws and all. I just enjoy loving me, even when no one else understands the road I traveled to achieve this decision.

Loving myself

Learning to love the skin I'm in

Was a dreadful dream that had no end

Each scare is a mark embedded in my heart

Reminding me of a life filled with sin

Of the life that I once wanted to end

MOTIVATING FROM WITHIN

Tears that I cried night after night

From the pain I carried in my broken heart

Praying to God for a fresh new start

With the reminders of pain written on my face

Thinking my life had to be a mistake

How do I go on to fight this fight

When the battle is me within my skin

Which is a constant reminder of the hurt I faced

Through past experiences that can't be erased

Only God can heal my wounded heart

And present my life with a brand new start

To replace the vision I see in me

With his glory and love to shine on thee

As my heart fills with his love, mercy and grace

A pleasant look now glows on my smiling face

His love now grows inside of me

LAVETTE WILLIS-CRITTENTON

Changing memories of pain to joy and peace

See God has taught me how to love starting with me

Removing the pain that dwelled within

He provided a chance to start again

See loving me was a lesson learned

And the beauty of survival was the gift I earned

So to all of you who don't understand what I say

Love the skin you're in it's the only way

The world is so different with loving eyes; I now see

How my life has changed

When I started

Loving ME

In summary, I hope that after reading Chapter Seven, Loving Yourself; you identify who you are on a new, more spiritual level. Some believe that people and things contribute to our happiness, when in fact happiness starts in our heart. Learning to love yourself is when you fill the void in your heart with the love of God, which guides your path to happiness. No person, place or thing can ever fill that empty space; you will forever chase a false sense of happiness.

Today, make a promise to love yourself on a spiritual level so that you may hear the voice of God directing your path. When you wake up in the morning, ask yourself; "What do I need to do to feel love?" "How must I support my happiness today?" We blame others for not making us happy when this is a personal struggle, so take responsibility for suppling love to your life.

Make a vow to love yourself even when others don't understand your actions. Loving you is a personal journey; you must heal the wounds and become whole.

Reflections for the Soul

As you reflect on the message in this chapter, be honest about how you might place your happiness in the hands of others. Recognize who you place this responsibility on and ask yourself why? You must identify your areas of weakness to take back control and regain happiness for your life in order to grow.

Loving yourself is a major component in the growth process of life. Use the skills you have obtained thus far to prevent what hinders you from loving yourself and release oppression. Challenge yourself to take control and be responsible for your own happiness each day. Review these thought-provoking questions and begin the process of loving yourself.

Reflection Questions

1. Have you ever told someone, "You just don't make me happy anymore" or said "I'm not happy being with certain people"?

2. Who are the individuals you hold responsible for your happiness?

3. Begin with a renewed mind. Start changing your focus by taking 15-30 minutes to sit in front of your mirror quietly every day and listen to your inner voices. When you're finished, write what your thoughts were.

4. Every day, ask; "Did I begin my day with a prayer for strength, wisdom and happiness?"

5. Every day, challenge yourself to say; "Today, I will be responsible for loving myself," until it becomes imbedded in your memory.

LAVETTE WILLIS-CRITTENTON

CHAPTER VIII

TRUSTING YOURSELF

Trusting yourself? What does that mean? How do I comprehend this short, powerful statement that starts with trust and ends with me? Talk about a completely new experience! The pressure of having to trust yourself can make you pop a blood vessel. Yes, I believe I have started making positive decisions in my life. The world looks so much brighter when you create a happy space within yourself. Completely trusting yourself means that you're able to make the right decisions regarding whom should be in your life, what career path to choose, etc.; these important choices are now your responsibility.

Despite the many areas previously identified for the healing journey to start, being able to trust the decisions you make may give you fear, doubt and confusion. Let me be the first to say that it is normal and will become easier with time. Throughout my life people assumed I had all the answers to my dilemmas, but I just learned how to survive and mask my problems. As I progress forward with a new heart and positive outlook, I look at my situations differently. Reflecting on my life, I visualize where I came from to where I am today and evaluate the areas that bring discomfort. I was living my dream right? I completed my degree, my children were doing well, I was interning with a wonderful company and I had my wonderful husband - what could be the problem now?

I grew up and now things no longer look or feel the same. I view my world on a higher scale. The things I accepted in my youth are not acceptable for me as a grown woman who no longer feels like a 'basket case.' This opened the door to new problems; I had to trust myself to make the right decisions for my life. I found myself lying in bed at night crying again, because something in my soul wasn't right. What I realized is that my marriage was a mess.

Keep in mind, at this point I had been married for roughly eight years and the pain I suffered over the course of those years was now taking a major toll on my life and my happiness. I started revisiting the steps provided in this book, forcing myself to re-read each chapter to realize where I was in the process of the marriage: 1) The mirror image - I asked myself what I saw when I looked at myself in the marriage? Did I like what I saw? Was this marriage a reflection of me? 2) The mask - How many faces did I wear as a wife? What face did I wear to display happiness in the marriage? 3) Depression - Is the marriage causing depression and altering my mood? 4) Acceptance – I am allowed to say, "Yes this marriage is causing pain and hurt, now what?" 5) Forgiving – Forgive my spouse and others who played a negative part in my marriage (including myself) and move forward. 6) Change - What must I do to make the situation work?

7) Love myself enough to know when my feelings are not being valued. 8) Trust myself to make the right decision. WOW. When I review the steps, I realized the process really works in my favor because I ask very specific questions regarding my life and answers concerning how I feel in each situation. I'll go just a bit deeper so you can understand.

Let me take you back to areas of my marriage that were questioned. When I got married I was young, hurt, in need of a family and love. Yes I had family members - but my husband represented security, affection and support for my wounded heart; things my family failed to provide. I no longer felt alone in the world, so we married and moved on. After we were together for a while, I felt like I was playing tug-of-war with his family for his love and attention. I thought some of it was normal or maybe I expected too much attention and it would soon pass, but I was wrong. It caused even more confusion because this is where the lying started creeping into the marriage.

My husband began keeping secrets attempting to make everyone happy, only causing more problems for our marriage. I talked to my husband and expressed my feelings of betrayal, which led to more problems. The more secrets he kept, the more divided our marriage became. It was totally disrespectful to me as his wife. I had no ground to stand on and my husband's support was gone.

I became just the woman he married. Our marriage was divided; my safety and comfort were gone. I had to protect myself because at any moment, the anger I felt from our dysfunction was taking a toll on my feelings. We decided to seek counseling and find answers to our problems. We soon realized we both were dealing with very unhealthy backgrounds. Shortly after all our lies - the trust was gone, which really through me over board. Dealing with the existing hurt and pain of betrayal and family issues, I could not handle the fact I no longer trusted the man sleeping next to me. I thought I was going to have a nervous breakdown.

My life was a mess and all these unhappy feelings started reminding me of the childhood trauma I experienced. I did not want my marriage to end because I didn't want to be alone, so I accepted this life as if it was normal. Towards the end of the year, tragedy struck as we dealt with the death of my stepson. My husband had to bury his son; all other issues became secondary while we pulled together as a family to deal with this unexpected tragedy. One thing holds true; death will either make or break a relationship. About a year after the loss of my stepson, our marriage really took a turn for the worst. I could no longer deal with being married and feeling like the outsider. I felt like I was sleeping with the enemy.

Consequently, I began acting out of anger and started living a reckless lifestyle; staying out late drinking and frequenting exotic nightclubs, as well as various motorcycle clubs trying to avoid the issues waiting within our home. I totally disconnected myself from the marriage mentally, emotionally and physically. I had no more fight left in me. We lived under the same roof however we lived two separate lives. My husband wanted the outside and so did I. I talked to my aunt and my father about my situation; something needed to be done to rectify things or someone was going to get hurt.

As our marriage grew more violent - filled with anger and hatred, I finally decided it was time for change, so I moved out. I got my husband's attention that change must occur. This did not last long; I think I was gone for maybe a month before returning home. Still battling our demons, we decided to attend church services and give our lives and our marriage to the Lord. This worked for a while; we began biblical counseling marriage ministries and bible studies. On the outside we looked happy - but tragedy struck once again when my father died and my world came crashing at my feet. I kept my 'game face' on as I made the funeral arrangements, but to be honest I was dying inside along with my father. Finally, I went into isolation from the world. I questioned everyone's love, dedication and commitment to me and it did not look good.

I no longer wanted to see or talk to anyone. I went to work and the rest of my days were spent in bed. This went on for almost a year. My husband and I were attending church our ministries, learning how to communicate and place our problems at the altar; we were starting fresh. At last, I found peace and no other events could fill my void; then BOOM, life slammed me again. The 'old husband' surfaced the day I received a letter that my house was going to be foreclosed on for non-payment. What?!

All this talking and counseling for nothing; my husband was still being deceitful. Then one day while in church, I felt something come over my heart and the pain was gone in the blink of an eye. I made the decision to leave my marriage for good. I packed up and left once again. Somewhere in my life I was told everything happens for a reason - so I must believe this too happened for a strange reason.

Leaving the marriage was extremely hard - mentally, financially and emotionally, because I had never been totally alone before. I always had my children and brothers, but now they are grown and living their lives. I still found myself lying in bed crying, but not really sure why? Was I still hurting? Lonely? Scared? Disappointed? I had to find my true feelings and I realized they were all of the above.

I had to believe I made the right decision and that something positive would come from my decision to leave, so I asked myself questions. What am I going to do with my life? What will make me happy and where do I begin picking up the broken pieces? Unexpectedly, I ran into a very old friend who I respected for many years and he began encouraging me to find balance and discipline. Therefore, I started working on me. I changed my mindset once again on a much deeper level of maturity. I began to strengthen my mind, body and soul. I listened to the desires of my heart, which prompted me to start a healthier lifestyle. I began to eat healthier foods, rode bikes, I learned to run, did yoga and worked on my book. I even enrolled back in school and started saving money.

I was beginning to feel complete as a person. I trusted and believed I could survive and make healthy decisions for my future. Many days I could not figure out which direction to turn because I kept hitting a brick wall. Through it all, God kept me grounded to make good choices to heal my heart and rid constant pain. Currently, I still have a relationship with my husband and we talk daily about reuniting as husband and wife. There are still many feelings of doubt and confusion and I fear our old habits will resurface because we have yet to address matters that drove a wedge between us initially. Right now, I do question my fears, my freedom, my security and my peace of mind. I wonder how much my fear of reuniting with my husband has to do with my experiences. I believe he loves me, however - I have found a sense of peace within myself and I'm not sure if I'm ready to surrender to a submissive life of dependency again.

The life of being a wife; how do I turn back the emotion and enjoy what makes me happy, while keeping the marriage together? Is the answer time? Does time really heal all wounds? Is this what the marriage vows mean, for better or worse? On the other hand - is this my sick way of determining his love for me by challenging his commitment to the marriage? So many unanswered questions, yet somehow I still believe I made the right decision by using the much needed time to take care of myself. Only God knows our future and I'm positive He will guide me in the proper direction. I trust myself enough to know whichever way I go - either back to my marriage or not, it will be the right decision for me. Even if no one else understands the choices I make, it's my life and I choose to be happy.

Trusting myself

Trusting myself is a challenge for me

Because deep down inside there lives a beast

Who holds my heart captive you see; she guards my

Life in spite of me; shielding me from harm and

Sorrow you see, that beast in me just won't go away

She rose to the surface and takes my place to protect my

Heart from a life of disgrace; no, I am not perfect and I will

Make mistakes; yet that beast in me will never be erased

Trusting myself because God has a plan, He laid the path

In the golden sand; trusting myself because He will guide the way

Silencing the beast trying to escape this day; trusting myself

Knowing at times there will be pain, yet I hold my head

MOTIVATING FROM WITHIN

high

And live with no shame; trusting myself to remain true to me

Trusting myself to keep my heart free; trusting myself to never

Live in fear because deep down inside Pooh will always be there

She is the beast no one really wants to see;

That horrible beast that lives in me

She is a part of my life and she fights to the end, the beast in me who has

No friends, her only goal is to sooth my soul

To comfort and protect the

Wounds and holes,

She has no love and she is not someone you want to

meet, she is truly a woman who belongs in the streets; trusting myself to allow God to shine bright and true Because if Pooh resurfaces I know I'm through;

Therefore, I'm trusting myself because I am smart beautiful and wonderfully made, by a creator who gave His life; so I may be saved

So I'm trusting myself this new creature he made trusting myself because yes I'm saved;

God spared my life He wanted others to see Now I'm

Trusting myself to remain true to me;

Trusting myself to keep God first

So my life will always have a fresh new start, trusting myself because I am just me;

Lavette Willis-Crittenton a woman trying to be Free

In summary, Chapter Eight, Trusting Yourself; encourages you to identify some of the trials of life that might make you question your sanity. You must determine what is right for your life. People tend to live their lives trying to make others happy and in the midst of that, we lose sight of what really makes us content. It's time to take control of your thoughts and trust that you have your own best interest at heart. Today, make a promise to trust what you feel is real for you. If you are hurting - acknowledge your pain and when you are happy, acknowledge that too. Begin trusting in you.

When you look in the mirror, say exactly what you are feeling at that moment or you will continue to suppress your feelings, depending on others for your happiness. Today, promise to trust in yourself for happiness by any means necessary.

Reflections for the Soul

After reading this chapter, think about the information as it relates to your life. Think about the person you display to the world. Be honest about the parts of your life you question the most. Identify areas of your relationship, career, children or your friendships where you need to take control. Trusting yourself is a major component for growth; start the behavior of trusting what you feel and acting on what makes you happy.

As you reflect on your image, challenge yourself to work through various strategies to build confidence in your decision-making process to rebuild the person within. I have listed starter questions to help you begin the healing process of trusting the person in the mirror image.

Reflection Questions

1. Reflect on the reasons you question your ability to make sound decisions?

2. Does this process have anything to do with the wounds of your past?

3. Believe in the process of healing, knowing you will no longer cause yourself pain. Do you believe you can make good decisions for your life at this point?

4. Do you seek confirmation from your higher power?
5. Make a commitment to challenge yourself to believe in the answers of your higher power; who you will consult before making any decisions for your life. Trust the process and move on.

CHAPTER VIIII

TRUSTING OTHERS

Trusting others, I just could not see,

Trusting others when they just hurt me

The pain that others placed on me trusting someone;

No that just can't be

Who can I trust with my fragile heart who brings no pain

only love from the start

Trusting others, you say it's a must; but who is worthy of my caring heart,

To give myself with unconditional love;

LAVETTE WILLIS-CRITTENTON

to trust a person with my heart and soul;

Trusting others will bring some pain;

but I prayed to God I may love again;

So the almighty, began to calm and tame this broken heart

To trust, someone opens new doors to a life unknown

To trust someone because all my fears are gone;

Only the Creator, my Heavenly Father understands

So He molds my heart and allows me to heal;

He makes me whole and I begin to feel

I kept my heart cherished, locked up and sealed tight,

As He drew me in closer; showed me a special love so true

Teaching me love and comfort how to trust only you

Wrapped in your arms was never work just a dream come true

All my tears you wiped, made my heart complete; my lover my provider my strength, my father my friend

having faith in my Lord is where my healing began

Trusting you first I will always win so my God I thank you, I have surrendered my life to you I have found my best friend thanking my Lord, I can trust Again

Learning to trust others is a daily challenge I will deal with my entire life. I have noticed that when you suffer from trust issues, it's like walking around with a glass heart. Have you ever tried to put broken glass back together? Let me inform you it is impossible. The fragile and broken, shattered glass is a resemblance of how my heart felt. I'm sure many can relate to the feeling of being heartbroken and needing to repair your emotional balance all over again. This is a process that takes a lot of time and an area many of us refuse to give adequate time to heal.

Most of us go from one relationship to the next, piling pain on top of pain, which keeps us vulnerable to hurt. Opening up and trusting others will always make us susceptible to hurt. This means we have to expose our hearts and let someone in to love us. In my healing process, I developed relationships with individuals I never expected. I discovered that I was a very territorial individual. All my relationships were strange and one-sided. I kept people close enough, yet far enough where they could only cause minimal injury to my heart. Well this process worked well with my friendships however, mostly my encounters with men were affected. All of my male friends wondered why I kept them as friends, could leave for years and return as if I never left. Nevertheless, most went on with their lives - but many let me freely return and expected their mates to understand I was a friend who would always remain.

I was their little 'Chucky doll', the friend to the end. This was indeed my understanding of them showing loyalty and respect. My relationships were very one-sided; I trusted no one, just me. I thought my plan was perfect until one day I reflected on some of the experiences in my marriage and how my one-sided thought process played a negative roll in it. I trusted my husband enough to go through with the marriage, but now here we are disconnected because I had no idea how to reconnect once the trust was broken.

Once I lost trust for the marriage mentally - I moved on, leaving a huge gap in the relationship. He wanted the submissive wife who trusted and relied on him for everything, when in fact I forgot that woman once my tears dried up. My protective personality kicked in; you know the one from my past, the survivor who recognized the struggle. I no longer needed honesty, protection or security - I had all that. Buried deep inside me, just waiting for him to make that part of me resurface and breaking the trust, was enough to release my demons full force. The relationship was at war; I couldn't see what the problems were, I could no longer trust him or return home to the trusting man I married. Today I acknowledge my part - as well as his part, in this marriage gone wrong.

I can admit I gave up on my commitment to the marriage and the vows I exchanged, I no longer honored. So, I quit on the marriage and moved forward in life because it was easier for me. I saw my past resurface and I couldn't bare the horrific memories of reliving a life of deceit and feeling abandoned. The story was the same, yet the players were different. I found myself having either really good days or really bad days; how do I find the balance of trusting others and not go crazy in the process?

I keep limiting my experiences to avoid any relationship that may cause hurt or pain. I pondered my past relationships to be sure I mended old wounds so they didn't hinder the success of the new relationships I encountered. Currently, I'm proud to say, I have a healthy relationship with my mother; she is doing well and we are learning to enjoy a mother-daughter bond. I was able to mend the relationship with my father long before his demise and I learned how to embrace the love of a father.

I also made amends with other broken relationships within my family; this was greatly needed for my growth. All of these relationships took time to mend and reach the stage of forgiveness. I questioned myself because now it was time to find common ground for my marriage. I still struggle with things we considered normal and it caused a great deal of confusion in my head. When I evaluate my existing relationships, I realize the only people I totally trust today, are my daughters.

This might be due to the fact they are the only people who never betrayed my trust in any manner. Surely, I can see the distance that remains in my other relationships. I sort of live life with the mindset; if I see them, ok - if not, that's ok too - life goes on. I now understand everyone has burdens they carry which become part of their adult make-up, so I guess this is a part of mine. So, I left my marriage - now staying on my own; one part of me feels fulfilled, but it's a lonely world living alone for the first time in my entire life. Some days I find it unbearable being all alone, night after night - I end up crying, reliving each painful event of my marriage wondering how I got here.

This was not supposed to happen in my life, not my marriage; my Cosby show lifestyle was ruined. I no longer felt his love for me was pure and genuine. We argued and fussed about everything; nothing was real. The devil was killing the marriage with my 'stinking thinking'. I became so closed-minded to his affection and his safety - I had to protect myself from the pain I felt. I needed to regain my thoughts; every way I turned, I felt betrayed by the people who were closest to me and I was very confused. Many nights I would sit in my truck, just looking at the sky for hours trying to get a grip on reality.

Some days I would sit and cry asking myself how, how did I get here. Other days I would just talk to my friend because I didn't want to be alone. We began to spend time talking about my dreams and passions, which led to him investing a great deal of time and interest in me. He began mentoring me, teaching me how to strengthen key areas which were weakened over time. I was learning how to channel my negative energy into a positive place. I was safe and trusted he would not lie to me or hurt me. While he was trying to be my friend, I needed something different.

I needed someone to trust. I needed someone to confide in. I needed someone with equal expectations - but they were never equal. He was giving the space and time I needed to recover and decide what I wanted to do with my marriage and my life, but I needed him to be closer, more understanding and more sensitive to my needs - yet he was living his life. This left me feeling lonely and abandoned again. My marriage was a failure, now the man I thought was flawless became a piece of drama in my life's nightmare. I felt like I was in the marriage because it was convenient and safe (my comfort zone), but I was miserable. Our lives were going in two different directions. So I really began to focus on me and not the problems surrounding me. I continued taking care of me and began to concentrate on the goal, "working each step of this book". My mentor kept me challenged to grow and push harder for what I wanted in life. I tapped into areas I never dreamed I would go.

I felt enthused and hopeful for what an adventurous life could be. He outlined specific areas I needed to stay focused on if I wanted to gain success over my life. This became my focal point and not my problem. I no longer felt the dreadfulness that was once draining the life out of my body. I found excitement and suspense, but that loving peace was still missing from my life - it just did not exist. I was never a part of his life. This was the same problem in my marriage and I needed to be held, cared for; the intimate conversations, the loving part of a relationship. I wanted the evenings and holidays I grew to love as a wife. I needed the emotional sensitive side of me to be nurtured.

Again, I struggled to trust yet another person who claimed to be a friend; the same way I struggled with my past relationships and it was so overwhelming. At this point I just needed someone to do what was right and be honest with me. I needed peace within myself once again, so I decided to separate myself from the drama of both relationship and remain focused on me. I said "no" to the marriage and the friendship; my job was to work on my happiness and do me. The betrayal I felt in my marriage shook all the past emotions from my childhood tragedies, leaving an empty void in my heart that needed to be filled. The comfort I found in my current connection momentarily filled the painful void. This is where my attachment and 'clinginess' came in.

It was much easier to trust someone else because there were no scares or battle wounds in my heart, so I felt safe to do what I wanted. I now had the perfect excuse for my actions. I was so intrigued with my friend he was tender, kind and affectionate to my needs. My heart was not looking for a friend, yet this friendship became a major part of my growth.

Once, I realized this process could really work for me - I was open to receive the lessons being presented. As strange as it may sound, this friendship began teaching me life skills that ultimately strengthened me over time. He offered a place of comfort, peace and safety - as well as security; everything I felt I lost in my life and marriage. I needed them both for different reasons; each relationship filled a unique void in my life - one emotional and one physical. Each relationship gave me a portion of comfort the other relationship lacked; I was able to give just enough of my heart without putting myself at risk for more pain.

I understood no matter what direction I chose, there would be some dishonesty - so my heart no longer expected what I would never receive; honesty, trust or faithfulness. At this point I just wanted to avoid any further emotional damage. What I realized, is that in life everyone we encounter will cause drama, discomfort or mistrust to a degree. However, I was stuck loving and needing them both for totally different reasons - but I knew my life could not go on like this.

I had to surrender and place my heart in one of the buckets of love and I chose me. As a result, I fell to my knees and prayed for God to direct my path and protect my heart. One thing my dramatic experience taught me is that since each person struggles in this crazy world with our own battles - we make decisions according to the baggage we bring to the table in a relationship. My dear friend was truly supporting me in every way he felt possible, he even knew when we just needed to pray he always had my best interest at heart. For me, it wasn't enough; I still need that loving 'end of the day moment' which says I'm here for you.

I had to learn to accept everything my friend could offer without expectations, which gave me the ability to embrace the life skills he taught me. Now I understand my twisted thinking is what prevented me from realizing who was trust worthy and who was not. We must understand each relationship will have different levels of trust;

however it's hard to see the good individuals present, when we carry so much pain from our past. We fail to understand we are not in the same roles our childhood situations presented. With this knowledge, we must view our life and our relationships individually and address each situation accordingly. At the moment, I have no idea where my marriage or my friendship will go from here - however, understanding this information, I know that I have two individuals in my life who care very deeply for my well-being and I pray with time I can fully respect and trust the love they give. I also understand the mental stress these relationships were taking on my life, so I decided to take care of my personal needs first and accept the blessing of having them in my life for whatever purpose my God sees fit.

To my husband; I ask that you forgive me for my portion of drama I contributed in our relationship due to my inability to forgive and my unstable emotions, I know dealing with me has been a challenge for you as well, yet you have continued to stand with me and I can't thank you enough. To my dear friend; Your Sweetie is asking for your forgiveness as well, for involving you in my emotional craziness - yet you still gave me your support, wisdom and friendship with all my heart I thank you and pray that never changes.

I finally understand that I can move forward with life knowing I have learned to trust God first. Each day I pray for God to direct my steps and remove any and all unhealthy relationships from my pathway. Therefore, if you are no longer in my circle then trust me - God did not see fit for you to remain in my life for whatever reason and I moved on. I instantly felt the works of my God working a miracle of peace on my heart and mind. I am able to take care of me and put each relationship in its rightful place. I know every relationship I have will remain stress-free moving forward because I am keeping God at the forefront. Prayer is my strongest technique for trusting others, becoming pain-free and focusing on my growth. It is how I will learn to trust others with my sensitive feelings.

In summary, my wish for you in Chapter Nine, Trusting Others; is that you identify those who are really in your corner and remove your distorted thinking. Some live as if everyone is out to harm them and that my friend is untrue. Today, make a promise to be open to trust those who remain true to you. When you look at the various relationships you face, evaluate the individual fairly concerning the good or bad they caused; only then can you make a fair judgment. Fear makes us not trust what others have to offer, however today the wounds can heal by praying for guidance and discernment regarding the people we choose to keep in our life.

Reflections for the Soul

Think about relationships on an individual basis. Develop a prayer life to assist with processing how you feel about the relationships in your life. Be honest about what caused distrust in the relationship and address it or you will forever have problems trusting people. As you reflect on trusting others, take notes and challenge yourself to understand how to repair the relationship before you let it go. I have listed starter questions to begin the healing process of trusting others.

Reflection Questions

1. List the various individuals in your life you are struggling to trust.

2. Next to their names, write why you feel there is a trust issue.

3. Identify these issues and determine if they are valid and accurate with how you feel.

4. Consider each person and issue individually and ask yourself how this problem relates to past experiences.

5. Now take time daily to pray about each trust issue with an open heart and mind. Focus on the individual and healing the issue.

CHAPTER X

FREE

Cry no more that's what I say cry no more be on your way

Let these tears be gone

let them fly cuz I'm free; let them tears be gone

Now the world can see, I am blessed in a way no man understands

I'm rejoiced in the Lord now I take a stand

no hurt or pain can make my cloud

turn blue no man nor evil not even you,

I kiss this pain goodbye and wipe my wet eyes for the time has come for me to fly; see I am blessed by the best;

God has filled me with joy; a bright light you see God filled my heart and now I'm free

For many years I felt my life was bound by my past. I struggled every day of my life trying to understand what a healthy relationship really looked like and what it felt like. All of the haunting memories from my past formed and molded my judgments and actions of today. My thoughts really shaped how I handled relationships, as well as my perception of self. This is where the work was needed in me to have a different view of self.

I acknowledge that we will remain trapped in life if we fail to look in the mirror at the person we are today - not yesterday. Yes, things happened in our past that we have no control over changing - however, what already occurred does not define our future. We have the ability to change if the desire is in our heart to do so. I must say that today I feel more confident about myself and my personal growth in life and in Christ. I read many self-help books and attended numerous trainings to help me understand some of the dysfunctions deeply buried within me and my family so that I can tackle the demons I wrestle with in life.

How do I heal the wounds and start a path in a new direction? How do I begin the journey to heal from these wounds so that I'm not damaging every relationship I touch in life? How do I begin to excel and love myself so that I can one day love someone else? When I look around, each day of my life I see young girls and boys, women and men of all ages struggling with these same questions.

Hurt forced me to search for answers within myself. I can now appreciate the fact that God allowed me to go through my turmoil and come out on top, still standing for someone else to see His glory in my life. God took a child who felt unloved, unlovable and unworthy and made her whole. Today - I stand as a strong, healthy and confident woman of God. I'm a college graduate writing my first book not for me - but for the individual watching me; that person saying "Why me", that person who needs a glimpse of hope to keep going on. Someone is watching me and seeing the glory of the Lord who saved me.

To be clear, I'm not rich with wealth - I struggle

everyday like everyone else, but I can tell you that I'm rich with spirit, knowledge, pride and joy. All my needs are met and every day I can see hope. I have learned to pray and remain focused on the heavens above, where my strength and inner peace come from. In return, I can see the footpath for my future. Being disciplined and focused on obtaining my goals and dreams are what have kept me grounded on the things which are most important. There are many times we point our finger at everything and everyone around us to blame someone for the wrongs in our life. However, when we stop wasting time blaming and begin changing - only then will we see the results of taking responsibility of self.

As the air clears, begin to analyze other areas of your life like your finances, your health, your spirituality, your mental state and your social well-being. Challenge yourself to change one day at a time and you will begin to attract a new energy in life. Set goals so that you can measure your progress and never be afraid of success. Acquire positive information about the desires of your heart for a different thought process (we are what we think).

Eventually you will find different places to entertain your peace of mind. Dare yourself to be different from your peers. Venture into those huge dreams that ultimately give you something to chase in life. Wake up with passion and drive; daily you will become stronger - allow no one to take that drive away. I promise you it works, I know because I am living proof that prayer, commitment, focus and determination are key ingredients to filling those unhealthy, unwanted voids we carry within our souls.

This is only part of my journey and some of the techniques I used to help me overcome my issues growing up lonely, hurt and abandoned. That was my past and now I have started a path to a different future for myself and my children. So I say to the individual reading this book - if it can happen for me, I know it can happen for you as well.

First, one must admit the mask worn is covering pain and hurt experienced. This mask covers shameful experiences one has faced possibly within a childhood trauma, sexual abuse, or abandonment and betrayal. Somewhere in life we picked up the mask to cover the pain. We learn to protect our feelings, but in order to fix a problem it is necessary to admit the problem exists. This is a process and takes time - a lot of time, really. In addition to time, you must be honest and understand the path of healing begins with the person in the mirror. My healing begins with me. I had to learn the process of being happy and only when I freed myself from the burdens of my heart, was I able to find mental freedom.

There will be problems and challenges in life but you can handle them differently with a clear conscious, knowing you trust yourself enough to make the right decision to handle things and move on. You can now take ownership of your life, your happiness, your dreams and your success - yes, it's up to YOU! Once you obtain this mindset then - and only then, will you begin the path to freedom.

Free

Like an eagle I fly high in the sky

Soaring the streets in search of me

Like an eagle I fly No one can stop me

Just let me be

Like an eagle I fly a silent peace within

MOTIVATING FROM WITHIN

Releasing my pain to finally live again

Like an eagle I fly

No more lies to be told, staying true to myself

And YES remain bold

Like the eagle in me untamed like a beast

Standing tall and alone in these harsh wicked streets

Like an eagle I fly

So everyone can see

This beautiful woman I have grown to be

Yes there was pain hurt and shame within me

But I let it all go, so my smile can show

No one will understand because this was meant just for me

I looked in the mirror at image you see,

Then removed the mask that shielded me

LAVETTE WILLIS-CRITTENTON

Lived through depression until acceptance came in

Learn to forgive my enemies and looked for change from within

Started loving myself and trusting me too

Each day I will try trusting others again

This will happen in time

So be patient my friend

Don't be mad I found peace within

No longer in search for my long lost friend

So for now I will

Keep nurturing this beast

Like an eagle I fly because

Happiness you see, I learned to just;

Let life be

Then I found my soul while searching for me

The eagle in my heart was healed again

When I learned to become my own best friend

Like an eagle I fly I just want to be me

Like an eagle I fly because finally I'm

Free

In summary, my hope for you in Chapter Ten, Free; is that you identify areas keeping you bound in life and release yourself. Many times people (including myself) lived life pointing fingers and blaming others for our failed dreams and aspirations which is incorrect. You are the only person holding you back in life. Today, make a promise moving forward to practice freeing yourself. When you look in the mirror, tell yourself exactly what you want. I dare you to dream big or you will never see change. Release the baggage in your heart and vow to free yourself. Change your mindset; it's the main ingredient of our soul. Good thoughts go in and good actions will come out; remember you will only get out what you put in.

Reflections for the Soul

Be honest about the desires of your heart and begin to live your dreams. This will put you in a position to work – however, it is also where you will see the benefits of all your hard work. It is your responsibility to identify areas requiring growth. Personal accountability is a major component in the growth process and a key element to being free. As you begin to reflect on your image, free your mind, body and soul to rebuild the person within. I have listed starter questions to begin the healing for releasing your mind and learning to be free.

Reflection Questions

1. Do you believe in yourself?
2. Do you want to succeed?
3. List 3 goals you want to begin with.
4. If you answered yes to the first three questions in this section, you are off to a wonderful start - therefore today, make a promise to yourself that each day you will awaken with a new mindset and repeat my favorite quote from the Bible; *"I CAN DO ALL THINGS THROUGH CHRIST WHO STRENGTHENS ME"*
5. Now I challenge you to set yourself FREE!

ABOUT THE AUTHOR

From a high-school dropout and single, teenage mother on welfare living in North Philadelphia, to a successful college graduate, author, motivational speaker and business woman Lavette has become one of the most respected and influential speakers of her time. Lavette finds joy in motivating others with her charming smile, gracious attitude and her encouraging words of wisdom. Lavette is eager to share her exquisite experiences of trials and tribulations that influenced the journey of her upcoming released book, *Motivating From Within; Possessing Inner Wisdom to Change.*

Lavette Willis-Crittenton is a wife, mother and a faithful servant of the Lord who has a great sense of focus, faith, persistence and determination to motivate individuals on all levels of life. She is highly passionate about education, personal growth through goal-setting and committed to new challenges in life. She is enthusiastic about sharing her gleaming qualities of motivation with you.

Lavette is available for speaking engagements and teaching sessions based on the 10 steps and guiding principle of her book *Motivating From Within*.

Please feel free to send an email to motivatingfromwithin@gmail.com for more information on booking.

www.ingramcontent.com/pod-product-compliance
Lightning Source LLC
Chambersburg PA
CBHW050642160426
43194CB00010B/1779